Conversations With A Half-Melted Tub Of Ice Cream At 3 AM

Debarchita Sinha

Dedication

I dedicate these poems to Life.
To the second chance, to breath returned, to mornings I never thought I'd see,
And to everyone who made them possible. To those who helped me survive the illness and brought me back from the doors of death itself when I already had one foot in.

These pages are yours.
This resurrection, yours.

Preface

In the quiet hours when the world sleeps but our thoughts refuse to, we find ourselves in strange conversations with memories that haunt us, fears that linger, and dreams that persist despite everything. This collection began before I knew what resilience truly meant, before my body became both the battlefield and the prisoner, before I understood that poetry isn't just about screaming into the void but also about listening for echoes that might guide you home.

Conversations with A Half-Melted Tub of Ice Cream at 3 AM traces a journey through **21 poems**. The first poems emerged from a place of everyday bitterness...the sharp edges of disappointment, the hollow spaces of loneliness, and the familiar weight of resentment. I wrote of trauma that "makes a grand entrance, with theme music" and of bitterness that "feasts on my insides". I believed these were the deepest waters one could wade through.

Then, June 2024 arrived, bringing a medical catastrophe that redefined my understanding of suffering. I was hospitalised with severe acute necrotising pancreatitis, which led to a multi-organ infection and a coma. Doctors gave me slim chances of survival, but I pulled through.

However, soon after, I developed Guillain-Barré Syndrome, which left me paralysed from the waist down, unable to move my limbs or control my eye movements. I spent months in ICUs across three cities, relying on ambulances for transport. I lost 30 kg, endured ventilation, a tracheostomy, feeding tubes, abdominal drains, and multiple medical procedures, including fluid drainage from my lungs and abdomen.

The final seven poems of this collection were written in the aftermath when my body was no longer just a vessel for emotions but a landscape of scars, tubes, and fragile victories. These poems don't flinch from the brutality of illness...the hallucinations post ventilation, the hospital nightmares that refuse to fade, the body that became "someone else's meal". Yet something unexpected emerged alongside the pain: a stubborn, imperfect hope.

I didn't set out to write an inspirational narrative. There is no epiphany where suffering suddenly makes sense, no moment where gratitude erases the trauma. Instead, there is the raw reality of survival: "I am no warrior, only wildfire's ghost, ash-kissed and smouldering, where forests once stood." There is the body relearning itself: "I am still learning the geography of my own body...like a traveller finding my way back home".

A friend once told me there are two kinds of poetry...the type that smuggles a message with a wagged finger and the kind that simply expresses the possibility of fighting through trauma without directives to the reader. I'd like to think these poems exist somewhere in between, offering neither lessons nor catharsis but more a chronicle of what it means to find language for experiences that resist articulation.

This collection doesn't promise that suffering makes you stronger or that survival is always triumphant. It simply witnesses the pain, the healing, and the strange, silent hours. If these words give voice to feelings you've carried silently, if they make the darkness feel a little less lonely, then perhaps that's enough.

After all, I am still learning how to speak the unspeakable, carry what cannot be put down, and keep walking when the path ahead disappears. These poems are my stumbling attempts at such impossible conversations...at 3 AM, with a half-melted tub of ice cream, holding on between defiance and despair.

March 2025

Acknowledgements

I want to express my sincerest gratitude to my family, loved ones, relatives, friends, professors, colleagues, and neighbours, who prayed for me, believed in me and refused to let the darkness win. I am especially grateful to my parents. When my flame flickered dangerously low, they sheltered it, fed it, and tended to it for its return.

My deepest gratitude is also to the dedicated medical teams in Jamshedpur, Kolkata, and Hyderabad, whose expertise and compassion guided me back to health.

I thank you all for not letting me die, for planting hope in my heart, and for instilling in me the willpower to continue when surrender seemed the easier choice. These words exist because you insisted I would live to write them.

Flavour 1. Traffic Jam Swirl

the blocks in my head stop traffic
(there is an inflow of terror talk);

an obstruction in the mindstream.
barricades set up by troops

(forgetting is a defence mechanism)
with mines and traps
for holding out the enemy

(memories from that night seep in through the bullet
holes,
leave their bloody thumbprints on the present);

at a point in the road covered by fire
(the crude sense of 'Being' in a maybe-existing world).

Flavour 2. Bittersweet Chocolate Trauma

My trauma doesn't fumble; it doesn't stutter.
It makes a grand entrance, with theme music, group
dancers, and mood lighting on the backdrop.
It will forcefully barge in on your white veil evenings,
But not before wrapping itself up in a scarcely covered
coat of Humour.
My trauma casually plays for you the voice clippings on
violence and death and the aftermath.
And it pokes, and it prods to get your reaction.
My trauma traces the scars on the skin and the scars on
the mind, and it demands to be heard.
My trauma says we're a team; my trauma talks of
bonding; my trauma says 'revenge',
And you talk of forgiveness.
My trauma screams, my trauma shuts up,
My trauma pleads to be heard.

Flavour 3. Smoke & Salted Caramel

We stand on the mutual ground of coping, but instead of
aligning as allies,
we bifurcate as adversaries.
I cry rivers of self-hate and our college floods in disdain.

.

I drown in my shadows, and you dance in borrowed
light, searching
for solace in a fog of our own design.

.

What if we traded our masks, can we bridge the
distance?
Find common ground amidst the chaos of our defiance?

.

You puff smokes of pretension and nothingness, and yet
somehow,
you're handling the split better than I am?

Flavour 4. Playlist Ripple

I've still got playlists saved for all my past people,
The ones who walked in, then out...
The ones I pretended not to care about,
The ones I pretend not to remember.

Maybe I drove them away,
Maybe I didn't mean to.
But once, they lived in the spaces of my life, and now
they don't.
You can't erase people, not really, not ever, not wholly.
So there they remain, etched into the contours of my
mind,
Only now, they've been reduced to music.

The first song she sent me,
The one I played when he was upset,
Or that song someone else offered,
But it stuck because it reminded me too much of them.
A late-night train song...high schoolers dancing, careless,
But I was hooked, it felt like something she would have
sung to me.

But what about now?
What about the ones who matter today?

Surely I should have songs for them too?
But I don't. I only have songs for the ones I lost,
The ones I wronged, and the ones who wronged me.

The mind is a funny thing,
It won't let me have songs for happiness.
And if it does, it only plays them when the moment has
long passed.
By then, the song is of bitter longing,
Transforming every instance of joy into a monument of
loss.

Flavour 5. Neutrality Neapolitan

the fence beneath me grows spikes
there is no such thing as standing still;
the roots wither in contested soil.

the privilege whispers, it's not your fight
we hear the sound of doors closing in other rooms

while newspapers fold into origami boats
sailing away on rivers of unshed tears
your silence has a weight that crushes our bones,
leaves blood stains and fingerprints on our generations
unborn

as seen at a crossing of comfort and complicity
your luxury of looking away while we cannot

the blocks of your mundane concerns
of Netflix subscriptions and anniversary dinner plans
fortify against our screams outside your windows.

'it's not political' is a lie
told by those who've never had their existence
legislated away like unwanted furniture

the myth of neutrality bleeds into tomorrow's headlines;

while the apathetic majority sleeps
in beds built on the backs
of those who never had the choice
to be anything other than a revolution.

Flavour 6. Self-Doubt Sundae

It's hard posting self-pictures that I do not end up
deleting within the next 10 seconds.
The mobile screen glares back at me, challenging me to
press the 'delete' button.

My self-doubts put up filters, stitch new traps for
holding out self-confidence.
Insecurities from my mirror seep in through the pixels,
leaving their muddy bootprints on the present.

True: Body shaming of any sort is despicable.
Also true: Thin privilege is a thing.

At some point in my mindless scrolling
I want to be liked and thought of as attractive and funny.

But self-loathing prompts work harder when you've
gained 12 kgs in recent times
Hyper-fixating on dwindling likes on posts, and holding
a hesitant finger over sharing/shame.

Who taught us the logic of measuring self-worth in
double-taps

While struggling with low self-esteem and anxiety,
working overtime.

Posting self-photos is hard, but my audience awaits,
Indifferent to the frames that cannot hold all of me.

Flavour 7. Holi-Stained Pistachio

When I was younger, I played Holi like it was madness,
If the colours on my skin did not linger past two or three
rounds of battle with shower and soap,
I had somehow lost.
I was the one who splashed herself first,
Who turned the bucket filled with colours down on her
own head, who tested the balloons on her own skin
Before launching them into the air.
I believed in my broken **pichkari**, which refused to work.
And the silver streaks on my neck and elbows were
battle wounds I showed off.
Grinning at schoolmates, strangers who asked, and even
those who reeked of ill-hidden disapproval.
I thought, **THIS IS REAL HOLI.**

But Holi is also a shattered mirror.
Each fragment reflecting a different truth, the festival's
shadow stretches longer than its light.
Let's talk about those who cannot consent.
The ones who do not laugh when their fur turns colour,
who do not chase after the hands that throw,
Who cannot wash off the sting of red and green.
Stray animals, left coated in chemicals, blinking through

the burn, licking at poison.
Let's talk about the hands that don't just throw colour,
but also grab, grope and violate.
The laughter that drowns out the **NO**, the excuse of
celebration masking the crime.
The women pushed, cornered, smeared with more than
just *gulaal,*
Their fears, dismissed with a **"Bura na mano, Holi hai".**

Let's talk about those who do not play but are forced into
the game anyway.
The ones whose faith does not celebrate Holi,
Yet find their doors pounded upon, their bodies coated in
unwelcome hues.
The ones just trying to get to work, to run errands, to
live their lives.

Let not colour be a cover for cruelty. Let not this festival
turn into an excuse.

Flavour 8. Déjà Vu Double Scoop

Every new person I meet has an uncanny resemblance
To someone else I previously knew.
It's like I'm stuck in a loop,
Where I keep meeting the same characters
In different costumes, with some other backdrop.
A stranger smiles, and I already know how they'll laugh.
A passing voice feels like an echo.
The tilt of the head, the hesitation before speaking,
Like muscle memory from a different life.
Maybe I'm retracing old steps without realising.
Maybe we are all fragments,
Rearranged over and over again,
Like the same puzzle pieces forming different pictures.

Flavour 9. Burnt Sugar Resentment

My bitterness refuses to chill.

.

She refuses to wear a sari,
refuses to go out with friends/family, refuses to pick up calls,
does not look pretty, might click pictures on self-timer sometimes
but will eventually decide she hates them,
refuses to put up a new DP, will heart react on every other DP,
refuses to let the envy show.

.

My bitterness feasts on my insides,
on leftover happiness of distant memories,
eats into details and leaves behind vague, disjointed images.
My bitterness, when it's done,
will stretch outwards and intrude on the happiness of all of you.

.

[I've been carrying this along for so long
I forgot how to let it go.]

Flavour 10. Blueberry Ink Drizzle

This is not a sad song.
You take pictures while I take note,
The blue ink dries on the spot as I spill more removable
colour on my nonremovable skin,
And the cats in your frame meow louder than my sighs,
And I'm not crying; I promised you I wouldn't,
But I take one finger at a time, and I break them, five in a
row,
And when I pause, I've stopped because it's still making
too much noise.

.

But don't get me wrong, this is not a sad song.
The stars in your eyes match the constellations I carved
on my flesh,
And when they align, it's like the magic we harvested in
our school days,
But like all the skins you outgrew in your youth
And all the people you left behind when you planted
yourself firmly on that train,
This magic weeps, and it fizzles, and maybe it dies down
eventually, but it understands.

Flavour 11. Revenge Red Velvet

Maybe revenge is the fancy new word you uttered thrice
in the last one minute,
While lounging in the comfort of your well-cushioned
sofa.
The television noise drowning out your better senses,
Maybe you felt anger before you felt grief,
And perhaps you use Honour and Condescension as
interchangeable words.
But death deserves more than a promise of more deaths.

In your dialogue with ghosts, what do you truly gain?
You plot your schemes of vengeance like a child with
crayons,
Sketching pain on a canvas of dead memories,
While the shadows of the fallen whisper truths you've
silenced
In your sanctuary of soft pillows, in your fortress of
distance, you brandish your words,
As the echoes of loss weave through your bravado,
And the price of revenge is paid in the currency of death
tolls.

Flavour 12. Death by Dark Chocolate

Death is strategic. It claims a body and in its wake, leaves behind a bag filled with fond memories, forcing you to shove your hands inside the soil and dig.

.

Death is purposeful. It brings peace and disguising itself as Relief, it eases all your guilt and the 'could have been' s.

.

Death is cruel, and Death is sudden. It strikes when you're unprepared and wrings out whatever remnants of dignity a body had left.

.

Death hungers and Death feeds; it pays us back in bottle openers and sometimes helps us drink down the emotions.

.

And sometimes, Death is just there, looking on with passive eyes, patient but hopeful, as we lock the door to our own caskets filled to the brim with leftover liquid, waiting for our turn and hoping to drown.

Flavour 13. Echoes & Espresso Chip

The voice in the shower is Angry.
He says I need to redeem myself.
My blades are not sharp enough for what He asks of me,
but I believe in penance.

The voice in the drive-through is Sad.
Says my silence reeks of Guilt and cancelled home visits.
She squeaks out an apology that sounds like a suicide
note,
Her shaky hands stifle every budding dream that dares
itself into existence.

The voice in the open field screams Disgust.
It wraps itself in every single self-hating bone in my
body, and boy, there are a lot of them.
It tells me life is an ongoing Embarrassment, says I need
to disappear, says I kinda already have
In so many ways in so little time that They barely even
remember me
That I barely even remember me.

The voice in the bed says it is time.
It tells me Hope has abandoned this heart.

He tells me Death is the Excitement of finally escaping
things.
That our Love was nothing but a momentary mirage,
That this Shame has stayed on for too long,
That no amount of Repentance is a good enough bargain
for the Forgiveness I seek.

He tells me I have overstayed my welcome.
She tells me it is time to end things.

Flavour 14. Bruised Berry Sorbet

I scavenged for love in dark, unassuming places.
With my brittle nails, I scratched it off the surface of my
sore muscles.

And splattered all of it across the space between his
clenched jaws and his fists balled up and waiting to prey
on a mouth they'd later call a liar.

It left bruises "on accident".

The "accidental" bluish/black/ purple/red on my arms
crawled along my neck all the way up.
Till it rolled back down my throat and formed a benign,
non-aggressive lump of denial

Which then settled in my stomach and (gently) thrashed
around in the dark
Howling (softly) and begging the "love" to stop (politely)
even as my mouth couldn't.

Flavour 15. Vanilla Stain Ghosts

the small changes in life accumulate silently.
after months of bad dreams leaving hollows underneath
my eyes.

that dark lane I would no longer walk down, not even in
daylight.
a little red scratch that murmurs its own story.

the shrill song of steel against the steel that holds my
spine.
the tragedy has passed, like silt in a stream, carrying
away pieces of the shore.

the grease scrubbed from the skin, the stain lifted from
the fabric,
but the flashbacks haunt me, resist this simple cleansing.

the grime is gone, they said. Move forward now.
morning arrives with steam rising from coffee,

water still beading on the skin from the shower.
I am clean now, I say. I am new. I am lying.

Flavour 16. Coma & Cotton Candy Clouds

In June 2024, my world turned upside down.
Hospital walls swallowed me whole,
Severe acute necrotising pancreatitis sinking its teeth
into me,
And before I could fight, the infection spread,
Organs failing, slipping, shutting down.
I slipped into a coma.

The doctors whispered their warnings,
Told my family hope was a fragile thing,
Told them I may not make it.
Yet somehow, against all odds,
I pulled through.

But hope was fleeting, a mirage in the distance.
Guillain-Barré crept in, stole the ground from under me,
Stole my limbs, stole my vision, stole my movement.
Paralysed from the waist down, I lay still,
A body betrayed by itself.

Months passed in ICUs, three hospitals, three cities,
Ambulance, my only vessel,
Thirty kilos shed like whispers of a life I once knew.

Ventilation, bedridden, tracheostomy, feeding tubes,
Scars tracing my body like battle lines,
Fluid drained - three litres from my abdomen,
Eight hundred fifty millilitres from my lungs,
As if my body was trying to empty itself of suffering.

Through it all, my family held me, anchored me,
Their strength the only thing left when mine had failed.
And now, I learn again, step by step,
A child relearning the language of movement,
The road is long, and the weight is heavy, but I am here.
I am still here.

I ache for the ones who did not make it.
For the families who lost what I barely held onto.
I have seen the headlines,
And I know, I know how close I came.
It is a miracle I am here,
Sitting, writing, breathing.
Life is fragile, fleeting,
And every step I take is a gift.

Flavour 17. Frail Frame French Vanilla

I do not think of myself as a fighter.
I do not think I am an inspiration to anybody.
I am the slow, painful climb of each stair, knuckles white
against the railing.
I am lungs panting after mere minutes of walking, a
pause, a surrender.
I am no warrior, only wildfire's ghost, ash-kissed and
smouldering, where forests once stood.

.

Most days, I do not like existing in your views.
You stare at my cropped hair, hair that fell out because of
the illness.
The tracheostomy scar in the middle of my neck burns,
as you stare.
The scars on my neck sting, as you stare.
Forced brandings on my throat, a memory of breathing
borrowed from machines.

.

I once said I miss my collarbones because I thought I was
too fat.
Now that I look like a bundle of bones, finally, thin
again, I do not like it.
My collarbones rise like ridges on a wasteland.

You should be more excited about fitting into old clothes,
I tell myself.
But they drape over me like ghosts, tracing remembrance
of a body that once held me better.
.

Too thin, like I could disappear any second. And I almost
want to,
Vanish from the gallery of your stares, slip between the
cracks of attention.
But I refuse to think of death anymore.
I fought so hard to live, and I will live, like roots
breaking concrete to reach the sun.
Like an ember catching the wind, burning, relentless,
and refusing to end.

Flavour 18. Hallucination Honeycomb

In the labyrinth of beeping machines, reality fractures
like thin hospital ice.

People dying and then coming back as reborn humanoid
creatures,
Translucent skin stretched over alien bones, eyes
containing universes they visited briefly.
Only now do I realize
They probably died in real life, crossed the threshold
while I watched,
Never returning from the void's embrace.

I remember thinking a doctor wasn't really a doctor,
He admitted he's an actor, secretly acting to be a doctor,
His stethoscope a prop, his white coat a costume,
concealing an imposter in this medical theatre.
I saw a nurse who wanted to kill me,
Her smile, a crescent moon of malice, stretching
inhumanly wide
Fingers hovering over my IV like spider legs, venom
collecting in the syringe of her intentions.

I saw after-midnight hospital parties, where they cooked

and consumed meat,
The hospital staff gathered like cultists around cauldrons
of malice, the ICU ward transformed into a
slaughterhouse,
As they feast on the flesh, the scent of iron and salt fills
the spaces between.
I dreamt my pancreatitis had been cured, and I could
drink juice again.
Sweetness rolling down my throat like liquid sunlight, I
felt the miracle course through me,
The parched cells of this body drinking deeply from
freedom's cup.

I thought we were in a game show, and if I could just get
up and leave
I could be free from the hospital, from the cameras
tracking my every move,
Freedom awaited beyond sliding doors if only I could
make my leaden limbs move.
I saw shackles and chains and they restrained me with
gentle violence,
Binds that will not let go, as I claw at the mask forcing
air into resistant lungs,
Fight the tube stealing dignity with every inch of my
own healing.

The room shifts between Arctic waste and inferno,

My skin could not decide if it was burning or freezing,
My breath crystallised before my eyes while sweat rivers
carved canyons into hospital sheets.
When I had visitors, they appeared like ghosts.
We shared meals in familiar cafeterias, conversations
flowed like on normal days,
While my body remained anchored to the bed,
unmoving, like an island marooned in sterile white.

I hallucinated all of this. Untethered from reality's
anchor, my mind
Created worlds within worlds, turning fragments into
coherent nightmares,
A kaleidoscope of fears and hopes projected onto the
blank canvas of hospital walls
Where the impossible became the mundane, and truth
was whatever I believed at that moment.

Flavour 19. Waffle Cone Paralysis

I could not move my toes,
(a null hypothesis of motion, an imperceptible data
point)
Just a twitch, a whisper of a motion, like the last spasm
Of something being devoured.

Waist down, I was an island
Disconnected from the mainland of myself.
(a case study in severance, a phenomenological divide
between the will and the flesh)
Night after night, waking to the prison of my body,
Half-eaten by paralysis, lungs tethered to machines that
breathed for me,
My screams caught, like a bird in a bell jar.
(a rejected manuscript, unpublishable)

Then remembering:
Oh yes, I am the subject of this experiment. I cannot
move.

Pain gnawed through my recovering nerves,
Like teeth finding fresh flesh in the carcass
(critical commentary finding fault lines in established

theory)
My body was a feast, where my immune system
Gorged on my peripheral nerves.
Guillain-Barré Syndrome – they put a name to the
glutton,
As it swallowed me nerve by nerve.

Intravenous immunoglobulin dripped into my veins,
(administered, like grants to underfunded initiatives)
But my vision split the world in two, and my eyes, once
free wanderers,
Became trapped in their orbits, stuck like knives in fatty
flesh.
The doctor's face: a map of fear, (a literature review of
failure),
As the disease crept towards my brain.

I became time itself during those sleepless nights, I hung
on that hospital rack,
(tears - the qualitative data of my suffering, pain - my
constant collaborator)
No painkillers, no sedatives, my inflamed pancreas
wouldn't allow such mercy.
Helpless as a fallen leaf, helpless as butchered meat,
Unable to turn to my side, unable to rise,
Wondering if my feet would ever again
Know the feeling of the ground beneath them.

Hospital nightmares still come,
Like ghosts that refuse to cross over, like a predator
returning to pick old bones,
(like outdated citations haunting current scholarship)

But today,
Today I walked 2.34 kilometres,
My tracking app counting each step, tallying the day's
cuts, except,
These were cuts I made into the world, not taken from
me.

I rest, then continue, watching children row across lake
waters that reflect the sky.
Hope floats like their boats, like spoons through blood-
red soup, rising like hunger after starvation, light on the
surface of possibility.
(like primary sources crossing theoretical frameworks)

I climb stairs,
Each step a mountain conquered, a bite taken back from
what consumed me.
I sit on the floor, then heave myself up, (rising with
dialectical struggle),
Like meat learning to walk off the slaughterhouse floor.

I am still learning the geography of my own body,
My body no longer someone else's meal,
(I am learning the epistemology of my own existence)
But I am hopeful
Like a traveller finding my way back home,
Like a researcher finding meaning beyond the
dissertation defence.

Flavour 20. Ash & Mint Revival

cracked lips taste like metal
the warlord's smile cuts deeper than
the silver of his poison-stained goblet

the witch's tongue drips lies
as my veins burn with each soft word,
the dark whispers of Betrayal's sweet kiss

breaths shallow, fragile,
shadows dancing on the pale bedsheets,
Death breathes close to me tonight

my grandmother's ghost
chants ancient protection,
and the poison turns to ash

scars bloom like stories
through veins thin as spider silk
tracing maps of what remains

the bones remake themselves
forbidden magic circles around the fractured heart
I rise, unbroken

Flavour 21. Toasted Almond Tomorrows

To,
The Ghost of Debarchita Future,

Are you still a lantern, flickering in the hush of 3 AM,
or have you let the wind cradle your flame into silence?
Does the moon still write letters on your skin,
or have you buried your nights beneath the weight of
reason?

I send you this poem like a message in a bottle,
ink bleeding into the waves of tomorrow.
Have you learned to read between the tides,
or do you still chase the shore, breathless and wanting?

Does the ice cream still melt in your hands,
soft as regret, sweet as a memory you can't quite
swallow?
Or have you learned to feast on the moment
without mourning its vanishing?

Tell me, do you still name the stars like old friends,
or have you let them fade into punctuation marks
on an unread sky?

Do your hands still shake when you hold something
fragile?
When you hold yourself?

If you have stopped writing, start again.
If you have stopped dreaming, dream louder.

With ink, with breath, with all the nights
we swore we'd never lose.

From,
The Ghost of Debarchita Past.